THE
SPORTS
DEVOTIONAL

THE SPORTS DEVOTIONAL

BRYCE T. JOHNSON

PRO FOOTBALL EDITION

32 Teams, 32 Lessons for Life

invite
PRESS

Plano, Texas

This book is dedicated to my beautiful wife, Jodi, and amazing daughters, Maddie and Mikayla, whom I love deeply. I thank them for embracing how Sundays in the fall are for church and football!

Contents

Acknowledgments

I praise God for His grace and love. I'm grateful that He allows me to experience Him personally, and I thank Him for how He leads and empowers me. I thank Jesus for being my Lord and Savior and for the Holy Spirit, who continually works in me and through me.

I'm thankful for my mom and dad, my biggest fans!

I'm thankful to collaborate on this book with co-writer Matt Osborne and editor Darla Johnson from UNPACKIN' it Ministries. Their gifts and skills are an ongoing blessing to sports fans and played a huge role in making this book possible.

I want to thank the board, staff, and supporters of UNPACKIN' it Ministries. It's a privilege to serve alongside so many wonderful people as we pursue our vision to see sports fans everywhere following Jesus.

Thanks to key supporters who continue to believe in the work of UNPACKIN' it: Mike Flanders, Patrick McAuley, Scott Absher, Chris Bryant, Mike Burch, Chip Pixley, Ray Hardee, Reid Fronk, Anthony Eshaghi, Griffin Gum, Casey Shannon, Steve Paulson, Scott Hamilton, Jason Ames, Tim Gheen, Scott Jones, Kevin Johnson, Kerry Johnson, Tim Biakabutuka, Brent Bowlin, Nathan Spang, Chris Blackmon, Colby Johnson, Graeme Keith III, Matt Barnette, Rob Rudder, The Rutherfords, Mike Allen, Brady Finklea, Ryan Saunders, Chris Efthymiou, Nate Salley, Norm Randall, Ron Laurita, Chris Cates, Burt Lohoff-Gaida, Rich Sedory, Harry Floyd, Rob Rogers, and Carl Zuckerberg.

Also, thanks to my mentors, Calvin James and Bob Schindler, who regularly pour into me and point me to Jesus.

Thanks to Len Wilson and his team at Invite Press for their willingness to publish this book and partner with us in such a significant way. I'm grateful for each person who contributed to bringing this book to life. The team worked hard, and I'm pumped to share the finished product with sports fans.

**To find out more about the author
and his ministry, scan here.**

Preface

I'm a huge sports fan who is passionate about Jesus. I enjoy watching sports, going to games, and listening to sports talk. As I do, God reveals to me how sports relate to life and the Bible.

God inspired the devotionals in this book by allowing me to see parallels in the NFL that relate to and connect to His Word. They are written to challenge, encourage, and inspire sports fans to follow Jesus and become more like Him.

In this book, you will find 32 stories about the NFL that parallel a biblical principle—one devotional about each of the 32 NFL teams. Jesus used parables and stories to communicate truth. Likewise, sports stories help clarify biblical truths for sports fans.

For the next 32 days, I hope you will read each devotional, answer the questions, and pray the prayer. I trust you will learn about Jesus, and develop a deeper love for Him and a desire to do His will. Reflect on what you read each day, read it with another sports fan to discuss together, and look up the context around specific scriptures for further Bible reading.

This book is for every NFL fan who desires to take their next step with Jesus, regardless of the starting point.

Day One: Did the Rams Deserve to Win?

Super Bowl LVI delivered a tight matchup that was decided in the final moments, as the Los Angeles Rams hung on to claim a 23-20 victory over the Cincinnati Bengals.

A few main talking points in the contest's aftermath centered around "deserved" and "undeserved."

Here are some of those talking points:

- The Rams deserved to win the Super Bowl since they went all-in on their roster and did whatever it took to have the most talented players.

- The Rams didn't deserve to win since they lost the turn-over battle and couldn't successfully run the ball.

- Matthew Stafford deserved to win a Super Bowl after losing so much in Detroit for 12 seasons.

- Aaron Donald deserved to win a Super Bowl after being one of the most dominant defensive players throughout his career.

- Joe Burrow didn't deserve to win so early in his career.

Sports media had fun debating these statements. But when it comes to our own lives, we all have a personal connection to the words "deserved" and "undeserved."

We can often act entitled and believe we deserve credit, accolades, awards, promotions, and blessings. It may be true, but when being rewarded for what we think we deserve is what drives us, we can become prideful and selfish.

With that attitude, we might even tell God we deserve His love and answers to prayer because we did something for Him. We may also think we deserve salvation since we are so good.

However, Ephesians 2:8-9 (ESV) explains, "For by grace you have been saved through faith. And this is not your own doing; it is the gift of God, not a result of works, so that no one may boast."

On the other hand, many people feel shame because of their past mistakes or low self-esteem, thinking they're undeserving of anything good. They feel like they've blown it and don't deserve to experience any blessings—especially God's love and grace.

Thankfully, the Bible tells us in Romans 5:8 (NIV), "But God demonstrates His own love for us in this: While we were still sinners, Christ died for us."

Ultimately, we must recognize that we deserve God's wrath because of sinfulness, disobedience, and pride. However, God loves us so much that He was willing to send Jesus to pay our sin debt, and He continues to pour His undeserved grace and mercy on us.

Romans 3:23-24 (ESV) declares, "For all have sinned and fall short of the glory of God, and are justified by His grace as a gift, through the redemption that is in Christ Jesus." And Romans 6:23 (ESV) says, "For the wages of sin is death, but the free gift of God is eternal life in Christ Jesus our Lord."

We are undeserving to receive it, but we must let go of the shame and willingly accept the wonderful gift of salvation.

We can maintain an undeserving posture in humility but should not reject what God offers.

I'm Bryce Johnson, and you can *UNPACK* that!

PRAYER:

Heavenly Father, I'm an undeserving sinner humbled by Your love and grace toward me. Thank you for allowing Your mercy to flow to me. Help me to remain humble and aware of Your remarkable kindness. In Jesus' name, I pray. Amen.

How can you cultivate a greater attitude of humility in your life?

In what areas of your life do you tend to struggle with arrogance the most?

What are some ways that you can be more intentional to regularly think about the gospel?

DID YOU KNOW

The Rams franchise leader in career passing yards is Jim Everett, with 23,758.

Day Two: "You Occupy Your Mind"

An exciting 2021 regular season matchup between the Tennessee Titans and Indianapolis Colts came down to a potential game-winning kick from the Titans' Randy Bullock in overtime.

Right before Bullock attempted (and made) his field goal, former kicker Jay Feely, who was working as an analyst for the game, described what Bullock might be thinking about before the potential game-winning kick:

"Just trying to not let your mind wander…Now it's just focusing on fundamentals, that's what I always did because if you occupy your mind it can't wander and think about the implications… think about well if I make this kick maybe I get a new contract… if I miss this kick we might lose this game. You can't allow your mind to think about any of that. So for me, it was head down, lock my ankle, follow through. You occupy your mind, you don't let it wander, you focus on those fundamentals and you make the kick."[1]

Feely's interesting description of a kicker's thought process can also be a helpful approach for us today.

When we follow Jesus, what we think about determines our behavior, attitudes, and emotions. Do we "occupy" our mind with the right things, or does our mind wander toward negativity and selfishness?

---

1. https://www.ninersnation.com/2023/5/15/23723503/jay-feely-jake-moody-49ers

Are we more focused on "implications" and what-if scenarios that lead to pride, fear, doubt, or worry? Or are we focused on the fundamentals of faith, which are loving God and loving people?

Romans 8:5-6 (NLT) says, "Those who are dominated by the sinful nature think about sinful things, but those who are controlled by the Holy Spirit think about things that please the Spirit. So letting your sinful nature control your mind leads to death. But letting the Spirit control your mind leads to life and peace."

Occupy means "to fill, engage, absorb, immerse, involve or divert." We should make it our daily goal to immerse ourselves in scripture, absorb the Word of God into our hearts and minds, and engage in prayer.

We must allow the Spirit to help us direct our thoughts to the right things. Then, we will have peace while our minds are occupied and focused in the right direction.

Philippians 4:8 (AMP) gives us this excellent challenge: "Finally, believers, whatever is true, whatever is honorable and worthy of respect, whatever is right and confirmed by God's word, whatever is pure and wholesome, whatever is lovely and brings peace, whatever is admirable and of good repute; if there is any excellence, if there is anything worthy of praise, think continually on these things [center your mind on them, and implant them in your heart]."

When we face big "kicks"—decisions, temptations, challenges—let's choose to remember Isaiah 26:3 (NLT): "You will keep in perfect peace all who trust in You, all whose thoughts are fixed on You!"

I'm Bryce Johnson, and you can *UNPACK* that!

PRAYER

Heavenly Father, please help me to occupy my mind with truth based on Your Word. I pray I'll focus on loving You and loving people. Help my mind not to wander toward negativity, worry, or fear. Thank you for keeping me in perfect peace, as I trust You. In Jesus' name, I pray. Amen.

How have negative and untruthful thoughts impacted your life in the past?

What untruthful thoughts do you tend to struggle with the most?

What biblical truths would benefit you the most if you thought about them continually?

DID YOU KNOW

The Titans are the only franchise to have had two different players rush for over 2,000 yards in a season: Chris Johnson and Derrick Henry.

Day Three: Faith or Fear?

Super Bowl LII between the Philadelphia Eagles and New England Patriots was among the most entertaining in Super Bowl history.

Yet, faith is the one word that sums up the Eagles and what they represented during their Super Bowl run.

Other teams that had faced the Patriots in the past had allowed fear to creep in and cause them to respond negatively. The Eagles, however, were a different story.

The faith they displayed combined poise, peace, confidence, and calmness. Nick Foles, a backup quarterback who became the starter due to injury, and Doug Pederson, a second-year head coach, boldly led the way by not letting the pressure of the big stage get in the way of how they approached this monumental game.

Not only did faith drive their demeanor, but it also affected their play-calling. The bold decision they made to attempt a fourth-down trick play ("The Philly Special"), which resulted in a touchdown, will forever be a part of Super Bowl history.

Similarly, another remarkable (yet risky) executed play occurred in the fourth quarter, when Zach Ertz came up huge with a fourth-down catch to keep a drive alive.

Instead of letting fear take over, the Eagles showed faith in each other, the coaching staff, and the play-calling. Most importantly, faith in Jesus was at the core of the team's leadership.

Doug Pederson, Zach Ertz, Nick Foles, and countless others were more than willing to explain where their confidence and peace came from. They accomplished an incredible feat but wanted everyone to know that God should receive the glory.

As we consider how faith defined this Philadelphia team, we should consider its role in our lives. Do we make decisions and have a demeanor based on faith or fear? Does our faith give us the confidence to "call for a trick play on fourth down," or do we always play it safe and fear failure?

Does our faith in God allow us peace when the pressure ramps up? Does it lead to boldness even when we're considered the underdog?

Hebrews 11:6 (NLT) says, "And it is impossible to please God without faith. Anyone who wants to come to Him must believe that God exists and that He rewards those who sincerely seek Him."

When we surrender our lives to Jesus and place our faith in Him, His power and strength allow us to do the impossible.

We don't have to let fear win when we're up against financial trouble, addiction, waiting, uncertainty, a health crisis, or even death. Instead, we can approach *our* daunting "Super Bowl" with peace and confidence.

Today, let's "step on the field" and go for it on "fourth down," knowing God is with us and that our faith is rooted in the magnificent, all-powerful King of the world.

I'm Bryce Johnson, and you can *UNPACK* that!

PRAYER

Heavenly Father, I pray I will live with an immense faith that unlocks Your power and peace within me. I pray I'll live boldly and confidently, knowing that You have already overcome the world. Use me for Your glory. In Jesus' mighty name, I pray. Amen.

What sorts of scenarios in life tend to cause you to fear?

How would your life be different if you constantly demonstrated tremendous faith?

What sorts of activities have helped you to cultivate increased faith in your life?

DID YOU KNOW

Due to a shortage of players caused by World War II, the Eagles temporarily merged teams with Pittsburgh in 1943. The name of the team was the Phil-Pitt Steagles.

Day Four: Something Is Missing

During his 16 seasons with the Chargers, quarterback Philip Rivers compiled an impressive resume that few signal-callers have matched in the league's history.

Rivers finished his career with more total yards than John Elway, more touchdowns than Joe Montana, and more Pro Bowls than Kurt Warner and Terry Bradshaw combined. He also played and started in every regular season game once he took over as a starter in 2006.

Yet, despite Rivers accomplishing so much throughout his career, people often overlook him when talking about all-time elite quarterbacks. Although he's thrown many touchdowns, put up huge passing numbers every year, and could end up in the Pro Football Hall of Fame, one thing missing from his resume is a Super Bowl win.

His contemporaries, such as Ben Roethlisberger, Eli Manning, Peyton Manning, and Tom Brady, all have Super Bowl rings. Unfortunately, Rivers was awe-inspiring during the regular season but couldn't fill the void of winning the big game.

Many of us have felt or are feeling something missing in our lives right now. We may have a strong resume that includes job accomplishments and amazing life experiences, but at our core, we realize they don't fulfill us, and we sense a void.

The truth is, only God can satisfy the deepest longings of our soul. We can have "great regular season numbers" like money, power, acclaim, and even the American dream—but none replace what's missing.

In Psalm 63:1 (NLT), the psalmist cries out, "O God, You are my God; I earnestly search for You. My soul thirsts for You; my whole body longs for You in this parched and weary land where there is no water."

Unfortunately, Philip Rivers was unable to attain what was missing on his football resume. In life, the good news is the emptiness or void we feel can be filled when Jesus is our Lord and Savior and our focus is on Him.

When we pursue Him with all our heart and rest in Him, we experience the satisfaction we're looking for. When we seek Him, we will find Him.

Psalm 16:11 (AMP) declares, "In Your presence is fullness of joy; in Your right hand there are pleasures forevermore."

In Psalm 107:9 (ESV), the Bible also says, "For He satisfies the longing soul, and the hungry soul He fills with good things."

Today, if something is missing in our lives, let's stop chasing after things that will only leave us empty. Instead, let's find fulfillment in knowing God deeply and enjoying Him.

I'm Bryce Johnson, and you can *UNPACK* that!

PRAYER

Heavenly Father, I long for the lasting satisfaction found in You. I pray I'll stop trying to fill the void by chasing other things. Please help me to remember that I don't need anything else when I have Jesus. It's in His name I pray. Amen.

What are you chasing after in life that is preventing you from desiring God as you should?

What difference do you notice in your life between times when you are passionately seeking God and times when you are more apathetic?

What would it look like for you to seek God more wholeheartedly?

DID YOU KNOW

With Dan Fouts at quarterback, the Chargers led the NFL in passing yards for a record six consecutive seasons from 1978 to 1983.

Day Five: When We Feel Unwanted

After playing well in his first season as the starting quarterback in Washington, Alex Smith encountered a life-threatening leg injury that caused him to miss almost two years. After 17 surgeries on his leg, Smith's career appeared to be over.

However, following an incredible rehab process, he completed his remarkable comeback by entering the game for Washington in week five of the 2020 season. In the games he started moving forward, Smith went 5-1 and won multiple awards as the NFL's Comeback Player of the Year.

But despite his incredible story of perseverance, Washington initially excluded him from their plans for the 2020 season, which led to Smith feeling rejected. He made these comments in an interview with GQ magazine:

"They didn't see it, didn't want me there, didn't want me to be a part of it, didn't want me to be on the team, the roster, didn't want to give me a chance. Mind you, it was a whole new regime, they came in; I'm like the leftovers and I'm hurt and I'm this liability… Heck no, they didn't want me there."

Smith turned out to be an inspiring football hero[1], but his feelings of being a liability, damaged, unwelcomed, and just a leftover are likely feelings we've also experienced. Sometimes people will re-

---

1. https://www.gq.com/story/alex-smith-nfl-comeback-player-of-the-year

ject us or not want us around or not want us to be a part of their team, making us feel unwelcome.

Or maybe we have heard the lie that God doesn't want us on His team either and believe our scars are too nasty or that we have nothing to offer Him.

Thankfully, the good news is that Jesus died for us despite our nasty scars, liabilities, and shortcomings. And He still loves us and wants us to know Him and be part of His team.

Romans 5:8 (NIV) says, "But God demonstrates His own love for us in this: While we were still sinners, Christ died for us."

When we surrender to Jesus, we are accepted and can have tremendous confidence in His love. If we start thinking we're unworthy and unwanted, we must remember that the King of the universe unites us to Himself. Even if others reject us, we can overcome that hurt because He has accepted us, which actually matters the most.

As followers of Jesus, the following verses fill us with hope, relief, and excitement about the truth that we will always belong and be loved.

Ephesians 2:19-22 (TLB) explains, "Now you are no longer strangers to God and foreigners to heaven, but you are members of God's very own family, citizens of God's country, and you belong in God's household with every other Christian.

"What a foundation you stand on now: the apostles and the prophets; and the cornerstone of the building is Jesus Christ Himself! We who believe are carefully joined together with Christ as parts of a beautiful, constantly growing temple for God. And you also are joined with Him and with each other by the Spirit and are part of this dwelling place of God."

I'm Bryce Johnson, and you can *UNPACK* that!

PRAYER

Heavenly Father, thank you for loving me and welcoming me into Your family. Thank you for seeing beyond my scars and mistakes, dying for me, and allowing me to become one with You. It's in Your name I pray. Amen.

How does it make you feel to know that Jesus died for you while you were still a sinner?

Where do you tend to turn when you face hurt or rejection?

How would fully believing that God has accepted you because of the work of Christ on your behalf change your life?

DID YOU KNOW

For 18 consecutive presidential elections between 1932 and 2000, a win in Washington's final home game coincided with the incumbent party retaining the office.

Day Six: Bucs Have No Rules?

Tampa Bay's convincing Super Bowl LV win over the Kansas City Chiefs was an impressive athletic accomplishment.

Almost just as impressive was the fact that the Bucs managed to return all 22 starters from their Super Bowl team for the following season. In a sports landscape littered with trades and free agency, such loyalty from an organization and its players is incredibly rare.

So how does this happen? What was the key to the Bucs' keeping everyone together?

This quote from head coach Bruce Arians sheds light on the approach that worked in Tampa: "Our players are outstanding. They do what they're supposed to do on and off the field because they take care of each other. We live by three words…Trust, Loyalty, and Respect…We don't have any rules."[1]

Interestingly, the freedom from rules seemed to work for Tampa because the players chose to take care of each other and desired to remain in that environment. Trust, loyalty, and respect resulted in doing the right things to have a winning team.

The Bible gives a powerful parallel about freedom and love in Galatians 5:13-16 (NLT): "For you have been called to live in freedom, my brothers and sisters. But don't use your freedom to satisfy your sinful nature. Instead, use your freedom to serve one another

---

1.   https://www.buccaneers.com/news/behind-the-buccaneers-bruce-arians

in love. For the whole law can be summed up in this one command: 'Love your neighbor as yourself.' But if you are always biting and devouring one another, watch out! Beware of destroying one another. So I say, let the Holy Spirit guide your lives. Then you won't be doing what your sinful nature craves."

We don't have to get caught up in a bunch of rules. If we love our neighbor as ourselves, we'll do the right things and won't have a desire to break the rules either.

The Bucs didn't use their freedom to do stupid things. Instead, they were motivated by their desire to win Super Bowls together, which enabled them to do what they should on and off the field.

As followers of Jesus, we don't use our freedom to sin. Instead, we're motivated by our love for God and others while the Holy Spirit enables us to live the right way.

Galatians 5:22-24 (NLT) says, "But the Holy Spirit produces this kind of fruit in our lives: love, joy, peace, patience, kindness, goodness, faithfulness, gentleness, and self-control. There is no law against these things! Those who belong to Christ Jesus have nailed the passions and desires of their sinful nature to His cross and crucified them there."

We can try to force legalism on ourselves and others or focus on love and "taking care of each other" as we yield to the Holy Spirit.

Jesus is calling us to love God and love people. When we do that, we'll stay on the best path and "do what we're supposed to do."

I'm Bryce Johnson, and you can *UNPACK* that!

PRAYER

Heavenly Father, I'm thankful for my freedom in Christ and Your grace and love. Help me be motivated to love my neighbor well and follow Your other commands. In Jesus' name, I pray. Amen.

How would living with a legalistic mindset hinder your walk of faith?

How can you avoid misusing the freedom that you have in Christ?

What principles could help guide you to best use your freedom in a way that honors God?

DID YOU KNOW

Tampa Bay is one of only two NFL franchises to be undefeated in multiple Super Bowl appearances.

Day Seven: Being in Alignment

Early in Russell Wilson's career as the quarterback of the Seattle Seahawks, the team implemented a run-heavy offense that focused on wearing opposing defenses down with a grinding and physical brand of football that featured star running back Marshawn Lynch.

Sure, the strategy was very successful for Seattle overall, but many Seahawks fans eventually became frustrated that Wilson was not being allowed to shine like they thought he would if he were allowed to have more opportunities to throw the football. They felt the team was stifling him from reaching his full potential.

Due to their desire to see the team begin throwing the ball more frequently, the fans started using a social media slogan that rapidly grew in popularity: "Let Russ Cook." They wanted to see the team give Wilson more control of the offense and for the Seahawks to tap into all that he had to offer and unleash him so the passing game could be more powerful.

The team eventually put the ball in Wilson's hands and relied on him to lead and guide them. The passing game became alive and thrived, with its MVP-caliber quarterback taking over more prominently. Their fans were pumped that the team had finally decided to no longer hold back Wilson and "Let Russ Cook."

There is a parallel for us as followers of Jesus regarding our reliance on God's Holy Spirit within us. Are we unleashing Him in our lives and depending on His power, help, and guidance?

Or are we holding ourselves back by not entirely relying on the Spirit and not tapping into all that is available to us? Maybe it's time we "Let the Spirit Cook"!

Each day, we choose who we "give the ball to" and whether we yield to the Spirit...or our sinful nature.

Galatians 5:16 (NLT) tells us, *"So I say, let the Holy Spirit guide your lives. Then you won't be doing what your sinful nature craves."*

Romans 8:14 (AMP) says, *"For all who are allowing themselves to be led by the Spirit of God are sons of God."*

The problem is that we limit ourselves when we disregard the Spirit's promptings and stifle or subdue what the Spirit wants to do in and through us. If we want to thrive, we need to be Spirit-led and remember these verses:

"Do not quench the Spirit" (1 Thessalonians 5:19; AMP).

"And do not grieve the Holy Spirit of God, by whom you were sealed for the day of redemption" (Ephesians 4:30; ESV).

"Now all glory to God, who is able, through his mighty power at work within us, to accomplish infinitely more than we might ask or think" (Ephesians 3:20; NLT).

Today, let's learn from the Seahawks, who finally yielded to fully embracing their quarterback's ability that had been available to them all along.

As followers of Jesus, we've been given the mighty Holy Spirit available within us, so let's hand over the reins...and "Let the Spirit Cook"!

I'm Bryce Johnson, and you can *UNPACK* that!

PRAYER:

Heavenly Father, thank You for sending Jesus to save me from my sin. I'm so thankful I now have the Holy Spirit living within me, and I pray I will yield to Him instead of quenching or grieving Him by going my own way. I pray the Holy Spirit will be unleashed in my life. In Jesus' name, Amen.

What would it look like for you to better follow the leading of the Holy Spirit in your life?

What sorts of temptations generally influence you to live according to your flesh?

In what ways do you think you might have grieved the Holy Spirit in the past?

DID YOU KNOW

The Seahawks were the first professional sports team to retire a jersey (No. 12) in honor of their fans, known as the "12s".

Day Eight: The 49ers' Mistakes and Right Decision

In the 2021 NFL Draft, the San Francisco 49ers traded three first-round picks and a third-rounder to move up nine spots, where they selected quarterback Trey Lance with the third overall pick.

Unfortunately, it didn't work out for Lance in San Francisco. He never developed enough to be the quarterback the 49ers needed him to be. As a result, the 49ers eventually traded him to the Cowboys for a 2024 fourth-round pick.

Tim Kawakami wrote about the situation in an article for *The Athletic*: "They took their massive write-off. They moved past the sunk cost. They owned up to the worst trade in franchise history. They absorbed the blame."[1]

He added, "The mistake was moving all those draft picks to get to No. 3 when there was nobody worth it. The mistake was taking Lance ahead of Mac Jones. The mistake was getting stuck on drafting a QB. The mistake was…everything. But it would've been an even greater mistake for Shanahan and Lynch to stick with Lance just to try to justify a bad trade."

Most GMs who draft the wrong players keep them longer than they should because they aren't willing to admit their mistakes.

---

1.   https://www.nytimes.com/athletic/4807005/2023/08/26/49ers-trey-lance-era-trade/

When they're too stubborn to say they blew it and need to move on from the players, one poor decision can lead to many others.

Despite the 49ers' initial poor decision, they realized it and eventually went in a different direction.

As followers of Jesus, we can relate to the principle of compounding mistakes regarding our sins. If we don't repent and move on, one sin can easily lead to more sins.

Sometimes, we make the wrong decision and make other poor choices instead of admitting the mistake. We might try to fix it before admitting it, continue in the sin by justifying it, or try to cover up one sin by committing another.

When we slip up and do something foolish, instead of denying it or pridefully making excuses that lead to more sin, we must humbly repent and move on in grace.

Proverbs 28:13 (NLT) challenges us: "People who conceal their sins will not prosper, but if they confess and turn from them, they will receive mercy."

In Matthew 3:8 (AMP), John the Baptist preaches, "So produce fruit that is consistent with repentance [demonstrating new behavior that proves a change of heart and a conscious decision to turn away from sin]."

1 John 1:9 (AMP) tells us, "If we [freely] admit that we have sinned and confess our sins, He is faithful and just [true to His own nature and promises], and will forgive our sins and cleanse us continually from all unrighteousness [our wrongdoing, everything not in conformity with His will and purpose]."

Sin can quickly compound if we don't admit it and turn away from it. Thankfully, by embracing the grace and forgiveness Jesus gives us, He'll help us live a life of repentance.

I'm Bryce Johnson, and you can *UNPACK* that!

PRAYER

Heavenly Father, I pray You'd remove my pride and foolishness that lead me to sin. Teach me to be willing to admit my mistakes and experience the fruit of repentance. Please help me avoid making decisions that compound the sin. In Jesus' name, I pray. Amen.

Why do you sometimes find it difficult to stop compounding sins?

How has your life been negatively impacted by a failure to quickly acknowledge and confess your sin in the past?

How can you better ensure that you will quickly own up to your sin and repent in the future?

DID YOU KNOW

Former San Francisco running back Roger Craig was the first player in NFL history to rush for 1,000 yards and surpass 1,000 yards receiving in the same season, accomplishing the feat in 1985.

Day Nine: Moving from Hostage to Volunteer

As sports fans, we're pleased when our favorite team drafts high-level players and love it when they spend their entire careers with that team.

Some players, however, ask to be traded when they no longer want to be with a particular team or can't agree on a contract extension.

Commenting on players desiring to move on, Pittsburgh Steelers head coach Mike Tomlin once said, "We can't do this with hostages, man. We need volunteers. We need good players, good guys who want to be here, and if guys can't check those boxes, it's probably best for all parties involved to go our separate ways."

A team has more success when players genuinely and freely submit to the coach's plan and fully buy into the team instead of reluctantly going through the motions out of obligation.

This concept of volunteers and hostages can also be a good reminder for us today. God loves us so much, and His plan for us is the best, but He's not going to force us or trap us into following Him.

He invites us to know Him and draws us to Himself, but we also have the freedom to go our own way. He's looking for volunteers, not hostages!

So, are we willingly following Him? Do we want to be in His presence? Do we think His team and way are the best, or do we think something else is better?

Another way of looking at it is realizing we're actually "hostages" to sin without Jesus. Thankfully, however, He offers us freedom when we submit and surrender to Him.

Romans 6:6 (NLT) says, "We know that our old sinful selves were crucified with Christ so that sin might lose its power in our lives. We are no longer slaves to sin."

Becoming "volunteers" on God's team and being set free from sin means we no longer have to be trapped, as described in Romans 8:7-8 (AMP): "...the mind of the flesh [with its sinful pursuits] is actively hostile to God. It does not submit itself to God's law, since it cannot, and those who are in the flesh [living a life that caters to sinful appetites and impulses] cannot please God."

We also have the good news that we don't have to be held hostage by earning salvation through good works. In Christ, we are free—we become "volunteers" and choose to do what's right instead of feeling forced.

1 Peter 2:16 (TLB) says, "You are free from the law, but that doesn't mean you are free to do wrong. Live as those who are free to do only God's will at all times."

Today, let's not go back to being a hostage. Instead, let's move forward by surrendering freely, volunteering to follow God's plan, and willingly accepting His salvation. Let's remember it's by His grace and mercy that we're free from the punishment of sin and now voluntarily remain on His team.

I'm Bryce Johnson, and you can *UNPACK* that!

PRAYER

Heavenly Father, thank you for loving me enough to send Jesus to set me free from the bondage of sin. I freely choose to follow You and surrender to You. In Jesus' name, I pray. Amen.

What would it look like for you to more fully surrender to Jesus?

What biblical truths might help you to be a more willing "volunteer" for the Lord?

How have you been blessed by choosing to follow Jesus and His ways in the past?

DID YOU KNOW

Although the Steelers are a storied franchise, it took the organization 39 years to win its first playoff game.

Day Ten: Our Biggest Foe

With Tom Brady entrenched as the starter, the New England Patriots won the AFC East Division every season except for 2002 during their nearly 20-year dynasty.

However, when Brady left the division to play for Tampa Bay, the AFC East opened up, allowing possibilities for the Bills, Jets, and Dolphins to emerge.

As ESPN's Rich Cimini explained in his article, "Jets Rid of Tom Brady, But Still Must Overcome Biggest Foe—Themselves," it wasn't easy for the Jets.

Cimini wrote, "Let's be clear: Even though they were tormented by Brady for 19 years, the Jets' No. 1 enemy over that span was the Jets. Brady beat them 29 times in the regular season, once in the playoffs. You can bet they beat themselves more than 30 times—on the field, in the locker room, in the front office, in the ownership suite, or all of the above.

"While the excellence of Brady and coach Bill Belichick contributed to the Jets' anguish, it's a flimsy excuse to say they were the sole reasons for the suffering. The Jets were mediocre because they were mediocre."

Former Jets' head coach Adam Gase agreed with that sentiment. He said, "We've just got to do a good job of focusing on what we have to do to make sure we're doing everything right in our building."

Most of us can relate to the premise that we must overcome our "biggest foe," ourselves. It's easy to blame others and circumstances for our decisions or what we've done with our lives. But finally, we must "focus on what we have to do" and "make sure we're doing everything right in our building."

Galatians 6:4-5 (ESV) says, "But let each one test his own work, and then his reason to boast will be in himself alone and not in his neighbor. For each will have to bear his own load."

Taking responsibility, embracing accountability, and owning up to our poor judgment are essential. When we do, Jesus offers us grace and a fresh start.

According to God's Word, we must embrace our new life and do what's right. Thankfully, we don't have to do this in our strength because when we receive Jesus as our Lord and Savior, His Holy Spirit helps us.

There's no need to keep beating ourselves up for past decisions. But we also don't want to "beat ourselves" with a pattern of unwise choices by giving in to our fleshly desires.

Proverbs 19:3 (NLT) gives us this truth: "People ruin their lives by their own foolishness and then are angry at the Lord." If we choose disobedience and selfishness, we can't continue to make excuses. So if we desire for our lives to change, we must surrender our hearts to Jesus, admitting we can be our own "foe" and repenting.

Today, let's get out of our own way and live a Spirit-filled life to experience fruit and victory.

I'm Bryce Johnson, and you can *UNPACK* that!

PRAYER

Heavenly Father, I pray I examine my life and decisions and not make excuses. I admit my pride and selfishness have led to foolishness. But I thank you for Your grace and willingness to give me a fresh start. Please help me to rely on Your Spirit to guide me. In Jesus' name, I pray. Amen.

In what areas of your life do you tend to make excuses instead of taking ownership?

How have you felt the negative impact of sin in your life?

How do you tend to try to justify your sin to yourself?

DID YOU KNOW

Jets wide receiver Don Maynard was the first player in NFL history to surpass 10,000 career receiving yards.

Day Eleven:
Cheering through
Disappointment

One of the biggest storylines early in the 2019 NFL season was the New York Giants switching from Super Bowl winner Eli Manning to rookie first-round draft pick Daniel Jones.

After an 0-2 start, Jones took over in the third game of the campaign and led his team to a dramatic 32-31 win over Tampa Bay. Jones played well in his debut, throwing for two touchdowns and rushing for two more.

As exciting as it was for Jones and the Giants' potential future, it was challenging for Eli Manning. Of course, he was happy for his team, and he knew that Jones playing well in his debut was a big deal. But he still wanted to be out there playing.

So how was Manning supposed to respond? Should he have been upbeat and found a way to rejoice with Jones, or should he have been bitter, jealous, and angry?

Manning was a class act, a true professional, and chose to be supportive. It would have been fair for him to be disappointed. But as he continued to find a way to embrace Jones and be happy for him, it helped with the transition.

Many of us today find ourselves wrestling with similar emotions. We lost our job, but our good friend just got a promotion. We're struggling to get pregnant and everyone around us has a baby.

Or maybe we're going through a brutal divorce while other family members are getting married.

Regardless of the scenario, there are times when we're dealing with a lot of pain while someone close to us is experiencing tremendous success or a joyous season of life. In those moments, we have the tough choice of either being happy and celebrating with them or allowing our bitterness, jealousy, and anger to take over and push us away.

It's fair to be disappointed when we experience something difficult. But it doesn't mean we can't rejoice with others for their wins. It's not easy, but as followers of Jesus, we can rely on Him to give us the power to do so.

Proverbs 14:30 (NIV) says, "A heart at peace gives life to the body, but envy rots the bones." We hope that as we cheer on those doing well and experiencing something extraordinary, they'll meet us in our pain and weep with us.

Romans 12:15 (AMP) encourages us, "Rejoice with those who rejoice [sharing others' joy], and weep with those who weep [sharing others' grief]."

When we genuinely love people and think outside of ourselves and our struggles, we are able to embrace them, honor them, and experience joy with them.

Romans 12:10 (NIV) says, "Be devoted to one another in love. Honor one another above yourselves."

I'm Bryce Johnson, and you can *UNPACK* that!

PRAYER

Heavenly Father, I pray that I genuinely celebrate with those experiencing joy in their lives. Please give me peace and strength so I'm not envious and can rejoice with them. Thank you for all the blessings I do have. In Jesus' name, I pray. Amen.

What situations in life tend to lead you towards envy and jealousy?

How would your life change if you were able to completely rid yourself of envy and jealousy?

How does it make you feel when other people genuinely celebrate your accomplishments and abilities?

DID YOU KNOW

The Giants played their first home game in 1925, falling 14-0 to the Frankford Yellow Jackets.

Day Twelve: Not about the Big Plays

As football fans, we love long touchdown passes and massive open-field runs. But interestingly, big plays aren't always necessary to win consistently in the NFL. Many elite teams implement a strategy with long drives, including a balanced attack of run plays and short passes.

Quarterbacks throw short dump-off passes to their running backs and quick passes to their slot receivers only a few yards down the field to pick up first downs. This game plan allows a team to set the tone by controlling the clock with long drives made up of small play after small play.

Drew Brees was a master of this approach during his career, especially during the 2020 regular season game in which New Orleans beat Tampa Bay 38-3. Brees threw four touchdowns to four different receivers while 12 different Saints players caught a pass. Interestingly, those four receiving touchdowns were only 14 yards, 7 yards, 12 yards, and 3 yards.

Brees finished with 222 yards, completing 26 of 32 passes and averaging 6.9 yards per completion. The win wasn't about big offensive plays but one successful small play after another.

What if we adopted this approach in our own lives? What if we consistently did the small things well instead of getting caught up in chasing the big touchdown plays that happened quickly? Rather than taking the approach of always looking for the "long throw down the field," what if we embraced a step-by-step process with "smaller plays" leading to significant results?

When we live an obedient life by faithfully doing many little things for the Lord each day, we keep taking steps forward. They might not produce drastic changes overnight, but we can slowly take steps toward becoming like Jesus and experiencing transformation when we "pick up a few yards at a time."

Job 23:11 (AMP) declares, "My feet have carefully followed His steps; I have kept His ways and not turned aside." In what we might perceive as a delay, God can powerfully work in us one day at a time. When we alleviate the pressure of always having to do something spectacular, we can focus on taking up our cross daily and following Jesus one yard at a time.

Psalm 119:105 (ESV) compares how a lamp lights up a tiny part of the path at a time to how God leads us: "Your Word is a lamp to my feet and a light to my path."

Today, let's make wise choices to do the little things God calls us to do. Let's take this faith journey one step at a time and remember, "The Lord directs the steps of the godly. He delights in every detail of their lives." (Psalm 37:23; NLT).

I'm Bryce Johnson, and you can *UNPACK* that!

PRAYER

Heavenly Father, I pray You'll help me stay committed to the little things each day and be willing to rest in You as I take one step at a time. Please help me be patient when things take longer than I'd like. Teach me to value small obedient choices as I trust You with the results. I pray this in Jesus' name. Amen.

What would it look like for you to be faithful in the little things every day?

In which tasks do you find that you have the most difficult time focusing on being faithful for God's glory?

How would narrowing your focus to be faithful in the moment help you to better glorify God?

DID YOU KNOW

The Saints scored a touchdown on the very first play in franchise history, as John Gilliam returned the opening kickoff 94 yards for a score against the Rams in 1967.

Day Thirteen: The Value of Adaptability

For about 20 years at the beginning of the 21st century, the New England Patriots built arguably the most dominant dynasty in the history of the National Football League.

How did they do it? How did they consistently win year after year despite regular roster turnover and their core players changing (besides Tom Brady)?

With the Patriots playing different styles depending on the matchup, the time of year, and the personnel, one theory behind their consistent success was their "adaptability."

They were willing to be a ground-and-pound team or would embrace airing it out. Bill Belichick and Tom Brady proved they could win in multiple ways. And regardless of their circumstances, they always figured out a way to thrive.

Mike Reiss once wrote about the topic on ESPN.com. In his article, Reiss shared offensive coordinator Josh McDaniels' quote from the "Do Your Job" TV special: "Tom, if he's supposed to hand it off 37 times and win that way, then he'll do it. If we need him to throw it 52 times, then he'll do that, too. It's the same way Bill is. Bill doesn't care if we have to win 43-40 or 13-10. The willingness to be able to do that is really a special trait."[1]

---

1. https://www.espn.com/blog/new-england-patriots/post/_/id/4818029/adaptable-patriots-plan-of-attack-in-2019-whatever-works

Adaptability means "able to adjust to new conditions" or "able to be modified for a new use or purpose." These definitions clearly described the New England Patriots over the years.

Being adaptable translates to our own lives as well. Life constantly changes, and each new season brings different challenges. With these changes, we can either be frustrated, stubborn, and hopeless or "adjust to new conditions."

As followers of Jesus, the way to be adaptable is to remain content and satisfied in Him, regardless of our season.

Paul gives us a great example of this when he shares his secret in Philippians 4:11-13 (AMP): "Not that I speak from [any personal] need, for I have learned to be content [and self-sufficient through Christ, satisfied to the point where I am not disturbed or uneasy] regardless of my circumstances.

"I know how to get along and live humbly [in difficult times], and I also know how to enjoy abundance and live in prosperity. In any and every circumstance I have learned the secret [of facing life], whether well-fed or going hungry, whether having an abundance or being in need.

"I can do all things [which He has called me to do] through Him who strengthens and empowers me [to fulfill His purpose—I am self-sufficient in Christ's sufficiency; I am ready for anything and equal to anything through Him who infuses me with inner strength and confident peace.]"

The Patriots learned to be victorious through their consistent adaptability. Regardless of our situation or season today, let's remember to be adaptable, always satisfied, and content in Jesus.

I'm Bryce Johnson, and you can *UNPACK* that!

PRAYER

Heavenly Father, help me embrace the changing seasons and understand that You're using me and teaching me differently in each circumstance. I ask that I adapt and remain content and satisfied in You. I pray this in Jesus' name. Amen.

What are some areas of your life where you struggle finding contentment?

Why do you think that you struggle with contentment in the areas that you do?

What might it look like for you to "learn contentment" in your life?

DID YOU KNOW

The Patriots are the third professional football team to represent Boston. The Boston Bulldogs were created in 1929, and the Boston Braves were formed in 1932.

Day Fourteen: The Minnesota Miracle

Fans who watched the Minnesota Vikings' 2018 divisional round game against the New Orleans Saints experienced one of the most euphoric plays in NFL Playoff history.

As Vikings QB Case Keenum threw a desperate yet remarkable 61-yard touchdown to Stefon Diggs with time expiring, the phrase "Minnesota Miracle" instantaneously came into being.

Down by one point and with no timeouts, the Minnesota Vikings were hoping for a miraculous play that would give them a chance to get the win over New Orleans.

Amazingly, the Saints' defenders couldn't deflect the pass or make the tackle, while Diggs stayed in bounds and ran down the sideline into the end zone.

You didn't have to be a true Vikings fan to start screaming and cheering about this improbable play that turned into a game-changing moment.

Sports fans dream of witnessing such unbelievable plays, and their love of the game results in heightened excitement. We watch weekly, play after play, anticipating the impossible. Then, when it happens, we are overwhelmed with exuberant emotion.

In many ways, our faith is similar. We wait and hope that God comes through for us, and when He shows up with a miracle, we scream and cheer in euphoria. We feel such joy and passion for God during the mountaintop moments of our lives because He demonstrates His miraculous power and love. These mind-blowing and faith-building miracles are spectacular and unforgettable. But it is also vital to consider what happens before, after, and between them.

As sports fans, we watch many games that won't provide historical plays, but we keep watching to be in a position to witness the next one. We see plenty of punts, dropped passes, and plays with no gain. But we remain dedicated fans even when the miraculous plays aren't happening.

Likewise, we're not to follow Jesus only when we experience miracles or are on the mountaintop. Instead, we must stay steadfast and committed to Him even during quiet times and walking through the valley.

Although we love celebrating the tremendous blessings in our lives and experiencing overwhelming joy, we must also be passionate and loyal between the "big" miracles. The truth is, every breath is worthy of praise and His constant grace toward us is miraculous!

As we reflect on all the past and current miracles and patiently wait for God to move again mightily, let's "Seek the Lord and His strength; seek His presence continually!" (1 Chronicles 16:11; ESV).

Let's declare that, "Every day I will bless You and lovingly praise You; Yes, [with awe-inspired reverence] I will praise Your name forever and ever" (Psalm 145:2; AMP).

Today, let's remember to "Rejoice always and delight in your faith; be unceasing and persistent in prayer; in every situation [no matter what the circumstances] be thankful and continually give thanks to God; for this is the will of God for you in Christ Jesus" (1 Thessalonians 5:16-18; AMP).

I'm Bryce Johnson, and you can *UNPACK* that!

PRAYER

Heavenly Father, I know there are miracles all around me, and there have been miraculous moments in my life. As I worship You and seek You continually, I thank You for every past, present, and future miracle. Help me not to take them for granted. In Jesus' name, I pray. Amen.

What are some small things in your life that you can give God thanks for today?

How do you typically respond when God is not working in the way that you had desired?

How would the ability to find joy in every circumstance change your life?

DID YOU KNOW

The Vikings have qualified for the postseason 28 times but are still searching for their first Super Bowl victory.

Day Fifteen: Are You Fast Like the Dolphins?

The Miami Dolphins were one of the best teams in the NFL during the 2023 season, finishing with an 11-6 record. They had an elite and dynamic offense built on speed, and their roster consisted of some of the fastest players in the league.

Receiver Tyreek Hill could top 22 miles per hour with the ball in his hands and was considered by many to be the fastest player in the league.

According to nextgenstats.nfl.com, Devon Achane and Raheem Mostert were the fastest running backs in the league in 2023, with both topping 21 miles per hour. The Dolphins also led the league in rushing yards per carry at 5.3, pointing to their speed.

In addition, the team's speed was a strength on defense, with Christian Wilkins and Emmanuel Ogbah combining on one of the fastest sacks on a quarterback during the season.

The Dolphins' speed on offense allowed them to blow past their opponent and quickly get down the field, while their speed on defense enabled them to rapidly move past blockers and be fast to the ball carrier.

As we consider the speed of one of the top teams in the NFL, let's unpack how being fast in the right ways enables us, as followers of Jesus, to avoid the wrong things by blowing past our opponent and quickly moving "down the field."

Here are five ways to be ready and willing to utilize speed:

- *Quickly Listen.* "Let everyone be quick to hear [be a careful, thoughtful listener], slow to speak [a speaker of carefully chosen words and], slow to anger [patient, reflective, forgiving]" (James 1:19; AMP).

- Quickly Forgive. "Be gentle and ready to forgive; never hold grudges. Remember, the Lord forgave you, so you must forgive others" (Colossians 3:13; TLB).

- *Quickly Say No to Temptation and Run.* "But you, Timothy, are a man of God; so run from all these evil things. Pursue righteousness and a godly life, along with faith, love, perseverance, and gentleness" (1 Timothy 6:11; NLT).

- *Quickly Give.* "Tell them to use their money to do good. They should be rich in good works and generous to those in need, always being ready to share with others" (1 Timothy 6:18; NLT).

- *Quickly Go to Jesus and Tell Others about Him.* "As the angel choir withdrew into heaven, the shepherds talked it over. 'Let's get over to Bethlehem as fast as we can and see for ourselves what God has revealed to us.' They left, running, and found Mary and Joseph, and the baby lying in the manger. Seeing was believing. They told everyone they met what the angels had said about this child. All who heard the shepherds were impressed" (Luke 2:15-18; MSG).

Today, let's be inspired by the speed of the Dolphins and acknowledge how we can thrive by quickly listening, forgiving, giving, running from temptation, and going to Jesus.

I'm Bryce Johnson, and you can *UNPACK* that!

PRAYER

Heavenly Father, when presented with the option to forgive, give, or run from temptation, please strengthen and enable me to respond quickly. Help me be quick to hear, slow to speak, and run fast after Jesus. In His name, I pray. Amen.

Of the five areas mentioned in this devotional, where do you find that you struggle the most?

How has an unwillingness to respond quickly hurt you in the past?

How might you take steps to be better prepared to respond quickly in all circumstances?

DID YOU KNOW

During the decades of the 1970s, 80s, and 90s, the Dolphins only had two losing seasons, falling below .500 in 1976 and 1988.

Day Sixteen 16: My God Handles That

Former Las Vegas Raiders tight end Darren Waller became one of the best players in the NFL at his position during his career. Waller was a reliable weapon in the Raiders' passing game. And in 2020, he led the NFL in receptions by a tight end.

But based on his success in Las Vegas, Waller was considered underpaid compared to other top tight ends during his career. When he was looking to sign a new deal with the Raiders, instead of holding out as other players typically do, Waller came to camp instead.

When asked about it, Waller told the *Las Vegas Review-Journal*, "I'm focused on playing right now. My agent handles that. Whatever is going on there is whatever is going on there. But whatever the outcome is of that, I'm here, and I'm playing."[1]

We should appreciate Waller's approach to controlling what he can control, trusting his agent, and remaining focused on his role as a player.

How different would our lives be if we operated with a similar mindset? As followers of Jesus, we serve a God who loves us and works on our behalf and for our good.

God knows what He's doing, so we can trust Him to do what only He can do as we focus on the role He's called us to. He cares for us, provides what we need, and fights our battles.

---

1. https://clutchpoints.com/nfl/las-vegas-raiders/raiders-news-darren-waller-drops-truth-bomb-on-showing-up-to-training-camp-amid-new-contract-talks

Deuteronomy 3:22 (ESV) says, "You shall not fear them, for it is the Lord your God who fights for you."

Exodus 14:14 (AMP) adds, "The Lord will fight for you while you [only need to] keep silent and remain calm."

We must also remember that Jesus fought the ultimate battle on our behalf as He defeated sin and death when He went to the cross and rose again. He tells us, " 'that in me you may have peace. In the world you will have tribulation. But take heart; I have overcome the world' " (John 16:33; ESV).

Instead of becoming distracted and worried over our tribulations, problems, and desired outcomes, we must surrender and trust that God is working on our behalf.

We must do what these two essential verses charge us to do: "Casting all your cares [all your anxieties, all your worries, and all your concerns, once and for all] on Him, for He cares about you [with deepest affection, and watches over you very carefully]" (1 Peter 5:7; AMP).

"Cast your burden on the Lord, and He will sustain you; He will never permit the righteous to be moved" (Psalm 55:22; ESV).

Just like Darren Waller left his contract concerns up to his agent, we can similarly release our worries, burdens, and battles to God by saying, "My God handles that."

I'm Bryce Johnson, and you can *UNPACK* that!

PRAYER

Heavenly Father, I trust You with my burdens and thank You for fighting my battles. I know You are working in my circumstances on my behalf and for my good and Your glory. I trust You with whatever the outcome may be because I know You are with me. In Jesus' name, I pray. Amen.

In what areas of your life do you struggle to trust God the most?

What do you think might be the root causes of your lack of trust in God?

How would focusing on God's past faithfulness to you help you to grow in your trust and faith?

DID YOU KNOW

The Raiders are one of just five NFL franchises that have a policy that prohibits retiring jersey numbers.

Day Seventeen: Chiefs Were Offside

Kansas City Chiefs

Late in the 2023 season, the Kansas City Chiefs were in a tight contest with the Buffalo Bills. With 1:25 left in the fourth quarter, the Chiefs had the ball down 17-20 and needed 49 yards for a touchdown.

The Chiefs put together a fantastic play. Quarterback Patrick Mahomes threw the ball downfield to Travis Kelce, who then quickly threw it five yards backward to Kadarius Toney, who ran 25 yards into the end zone for a touchdown.

It was unbelievably exciting until everyone realized there was a flag on the play. Toney was penalized for being offside and not lining up behind the ball.

Unfortunately, Toney was too far past the line and didn't appear to look at the ref to make sure he was where he needed to be.

Following the game, referee Carl Cheffers said, "Yes, ultimately, if they looked for alignment advice, certainly we are going to give it to them."[1] Toney could have avoided the penalty and been a hero for scoring the touchdown. But instead, he cost his team by not making sure he was aligned correctly.

1. https://chiefsdigest.com/chiefs-complain-officials-explain-after-offsides-call-erases-kcs-crazy-touchdown/

It's too bad such an avoidable penalty overshadowed the game, but there's an important parallel for us to consider regarding our lives. Here are some questions for us to consider:

- Do we desire to be aligned with God's will?
- Do we look to God to ensure we're correctly lined up before "running down the field?"
- Do we know God's Word so we can discern whether or not we're crossing the line?

Ephesians 5:15-17 (AMP) says, "Therefore see that you walk carefully [living life with honor, purpose, and courage; shunning those who tolerate and enable evil], not as the unwise, but as wise [sensible, intelligent, discerning people], making the very most of your time [on earth, recognizing and taking advantage of each opportunity and using it with wisdom and diligence], because the days are [filled with] evil. Therefore do not be foolish and thoughtless, but understand and firmly grasp what the will of the Lord is."

Just like the ref was willing to give "alignment advice," God is willing to provide us with "alignment advice" when we look to Him. He doesn't want us to cross the line into sin but to remain where we need to be—right in His will.

We must turn to God and pray Psalm 143:10 (NLT): "Teach me to do Your will, for You are my God. May Your gracious Spirit lead me forward on a firm footing."

Sometimes, we can score an "amazing touchdown." But if we "cross the line" along the way, it's not going to stand for long.

So today, let's avoid being "offside" and adequately align ourselves with God and His Word as we ask Him to guide our steps.

I'm Bryce Johnson, and you can *UNPACK* that!

PRAYER

Heavenly Father, I desire to do Your will and remain aligned with You. I pray that I will continue to know Your Word more and follow wherever You guide me. Help me not to cross the line or try to get ahead of You in any way but rather stay lined up with Your plan. In Jesus' name, I pray. Amen.

What is one biblical topic or subject in which you need to grow in your understanding?

What are some ways you might be able to better assess how you are aligning with God's desires for your life?

What are some areas of your life where you know that you are not currently aligned with God's desires for you?

DID YOU KNOW

The Kansas City record for most passing yards in a single game is held by Elvis Grbac, who threw for 504 yards during a regular season contest in 2000.

Day Eighteen: Patience and a Comeback

The 2022 NFL wildcard round gave us one of the most unique and exciting playoff games in league history. Playing on the road in Jacksonville, the Los Angeles Chargers jumped out to a 27-0 first-half lead over the home team.

The Jaguars' chances of winning the game appeared improbable with that deficit in front of them. However, they shocked everyone and put together the third-largest comeback in playoff history, winning 31-30.

So how did a team put together a remarkable comeback like that when losing 27-0?

The first step was embracing the daunting reality that they couldn't score 27 points all at once. It was going to take time to chip away at the lead. Jacksonville had to stick to the principle of taking it one play at a time and keeping the faith with perseverance until the end.

As followers of Jesus, we desire to seek God and grow spiritually, but we know we have a long way to go. We want to mature in our faith, understand scripture, and develop our character to be more like Jesus. Yet we want it to happen overnight.

In reality, following Jesus is a journey that requires one step at a time. He chips away and refines us a little bit at a time as we trust Him. We gain wisdom and understanding as we read God's Word one verse at a time.

The growing process and the patience required are also evident in agriculture, which is why Jesus spoke about it in many of His parables. In the "Parable of the Sower" in Luke 8, Jesus speaks about a sower sowing seed and describes four ways the soil reacts to the seeds.

Jesus explains, "The seed is the Word of God" (Luke 8:11; ESV). In verse 15 (AMP), He further explains, "But as for that seed in the good soil, these are the ones who have heard the Word with a good and noble heart, and hold on to it tightly, and bear fruit with patience."

Luke 8:15 in the New Living Translation says, "And the seeds that fell on the good soil represent honest, good-hearted people who hear God's Word, cling to it, and patiently produce a huge harvest."

Today, let's be encouraged to continue valuing God's Word by deeply rooting it in our hearts and holding it tightly. When we do, we will patiently experience the fruit of persevering in faith.

Let's take a patient approach to spiritual maturity and reading God's Word. We won't be able to close the gap entirely in an instant. Still, as we diligently take incremental steps toward becoming more like Jesus, we can be confident that He will ultimately help bring about the fruit in His perfect timing.

I'm Bryce Johnson, and you can *UNPACK* that!

PRAYER

Heavenly Father, thank you for giving me Your Word. It changes me, my character, my thoughts, and my perspectives. I pray I will cling to You and Your Word with patience, knowing that fruit and a harvest will come in time as I persevere. In Jesus' name, I pray. Amen.

How might you be able to remain encouraged even when you don't notice significant spiritual growth taking place in your life?

How have you seen the buildup of incremental growth lead to a major change in your life?

What are some areas of your life where you need to be more intentional about working toward incremental growth?

DID YOU KNOW

Jacksonville's team nickname was selected because the Jacksonville Zoo owned the oldest living jaguar in North America at the time.

Day Nineteen: Decision Interceptions

Indianapolis Colts

Andrew Luck was once a star quarterback in the NFL, putting together some impressive seasons with the Colts. However, he struggled with interceptions for a decent portion of his career.

We know how important it is for quarterbacks to protect the ball and not throw interceptions. But we also know that quarterbacks aren't perfect. Even the best ones will throw a few picks throughout the season.

As Luck worked to reduce his interception totals, his quarterback coach Brian Schottenheimer explained, "We say this all the time, 'Andrew should not be a double-digit interception guy.' Like, that's the phrase that we use. He's just too good of a player. So again, if he can eliminate some of those decision interceptions—I think there are five or six of them—those numbers drop significantly. You're going to throw interceptions. It just happens."

Luck had to work on his decision-making and not throw passes when he knew it would be dangerous. He put himself and those around him in a tough spot when he regularly went against what he knew deep down was best and threw an unwise pass.

We know none of us are perfect, and we won't make the "right throw" every time. However, as we study scripture and follow Jesus, we realize which situations and sins to avoid.

We must become aware of our "decision interceptions"—which times we're likely to give into temptation or continue a pattern of sin that we know is in direct disobedience to God. In other words, we must recognize when we're about to choose to go against what we know is best.

We must listen to our "coach" and trust Him to help us overcome the "decision interceptions." As we grow in our faith and wisdom and rely on the Holy Spirit, there will be fewer and fewer times we willingly do what we know we shouldn't.

1 John 3:9 (AMP) tells us, "No one who is born of God [deliberately, knowingly, and habitually] practices sin, because God's seed [His principle of life, the essence of His righteous character] remains [permanently] in him [who is born again—who is reborn from above—spiritually transformed, renewed, and set apart for His purpose]; and he [who is born again] cannot habitually [live a life characterized by] sin, because he is born of God and longs to please Him."

1 John 3:6 (AMP) says, "No one who abides in Him [who remains united in fellowship with Him—deliberately, knowingly, and habitually] practices sin. No one who habitually sins has seen Him or known Him."

When we truly surrender and follow Jesus moment by moment, He gives us the wisdom and understanding to see the field clearly and avoid the situations and "decision interceptions" we no longer have to make.

I'm Bryce Johnson, and you can *UNPACK* that!

PRAYER

Heavenly Father, please help me to realize the sin in my life that I need to surrender. Give me the strength to walk in Your ways and move on from the sin that I no longer need to choose. In Jesus' name, I pray. Amen.

What are some scenarios and circumstances that tend to lead you into temptations?

What changes might you need to make in your life in order to ensure that you are not placing yourself in position to easily be tempted?

Why do you think you sometimes put yourself into positions where you know you will be tempted to sin?

DID YOU KNOW

In 2003, Colts kicker Mike Vanderjagt became the first kicker in NFL history to play an entire regular season and postseason without missing a field goal or extra point.

Day Twenty: 9-7 Is Not the Bar

Houston Texans

It's safe to say that each NFL team has goals they are trying to reach in any given season, whether winning a few more games than the year before, making the playoffs, or going to the Super Bowl. No matter the organization, there are expectations and standards that teams hope to achieve throughout the year.

Though Bill O'Brien had a relatively successful tenure as the head coach of the Houston Texans, many fans grew tired of the fact that the team seemed stuck in a state of being pretty good but not great. After going 9-7 in both of his first two seasons with the team, this is what O'Brien said before his third season started:

"We understand that 9-7 is not the bar. We feel like we've made some really good strides here in the past two years with our football team. We've overcome some adversity. We have a mentally tough team. We've got a bunch of great guys in that locker room, but we know that the 9-7 bar is too low. We understand that. I think everybody in this league understands that. We're very well aware of the fact that we need to go out there and play more consistent, play better than we have in the past. But that is in the past. This is a new team, and I really like the way this team is practicing. We'll go from there."[1]

---

1. https://www.nbcsports.com/nfl/profootballtalk/rumor-mill/news/colts-tell-andrew-luck-not-to-be-a-double-digit-interception-guy

O'Brien's mentality parallels well to our approach to the standard we should have as followers of Jesus. We can no longer settle for being like we were in the past or living like the rest of the world. The bar is set much higher for us, and we can't settle for just being "9-7" by not taking steps to become more and more like Jesus each day. We rest in His grace as we recognize He's the benchmark for how to live.

In 1 Peter 1:13-16 (NLT), the Bible says, "So prepare your minds for action and exercise self-control. Put all your hope in the gracious salvation that will come to you when Jesus Christ is revealed to the world. So, you must live as God's obedient children. Don't slip back into your old ways of living to satisfy your own desires. You didn't know any better then. But now you must be holy in everything you do, just as God who chose you is holy. For the Scriptures say, 'You must be holy because I am holy.'"

As followers of Jesus, we seek holiness and to be different from the rest of the world. Today, let's not settle for being the same as we were last year or even yesterday. Through God's transforming power, let's grow and live according to His standards.

I'm Bryce Johnson, and you can *UNPACK* that!

PRAYER

Heavenly Father, you are Holy and wonderful. I pray that You give me the strength to seek holiness in the way I live my life. I want to be different and know You hold me to a higher standard. Show me how to raise the bar and become set apart from the world as I trust and follow You. In Jesus' name, I pray. Amen.

In what areas of your life do you think you might have grown complacent and stopped fighting for growth?

How would regularly focusing on God's standards help keep you motivated to continue growing in your faith and character?

How might comparing yourself with other people cause you to miss out on the life that God has for you?

DID YOU KNOW

Texans quarterback C.J. Stroud is the youngest signal caller to win an NFL playoff game, having done so at 22 years and 102 days.

Day Twenty-One: "My Future Is a Beautiful Mystery"

Despite winning an NFL MVP when Aaron Rodgers was 37, fans and the media began wondering about his future with the Green Bay Packers after the team drafted younger quarterback Jordan Love in the first round of the previous year's NFL draft.

Even so, Rodgers wasn't focused on their concerns when he commented during an interview with ESPN.com before the NFC Championship Game: "I'm always just trying to stay present, especially this year, as much as anything, and enjoy the moments. I hope there's more opportunities, but I don't know. I mean, I really don't. That stuff is out of my control. My future is a beautiful mystery, I think."

He explained further, "All that other stuff…is stuff that I'm just not going to focus on. Because to me, it is a beautiful mystery what happens down the line, but there'll be a time when we meet that future, and right now, I'm just going to enjoy the present."[1]

All of us today have questions about what will happen in the future. These questions can easily take our focus away from the present and keep us from making the most of the moments we're experiencing right now.

---

1. https://www.espn.com/nfl/story/_/id/30749615/green-bay-packers-qb-aaron-rodgers-says-future-beautiful-mystery

Gratitude and peace are difficult to achieve when we concentrate too much on the future and worry about the unknown. However, as followers of Jesus, we can abound in hope because we know God is in charge and that our future is eternity with Him.

This assurance allows us to soak in the moment, know who's in control, enjoy God's presence in the present, and not worry about what happens down the line.

The Bible encourages us in Matthew 6:33-34 (NLT) to "Seek the Kingdom of God above all else, and live righteously, and He will give you everything you need. So don't worry about tomorrow, for tomorrow will bring its own worries. Today's trouble is enough for today."

Similarly, Luke 12:31-32 (AMP) says, "But [strive for and actively] seek His kingdom, and these things will be given to you as well. Do not be afraid and anxious, little flock, for it is your Father's good pleasure to give you the kingdom."

Lastly, as we long for Jesus to return to earth and take us home, let's remember we don't know when He's coming back, but in the meantime, we can embrace that "beautiful mystery."

As Matthew 24:42 (AMP) tells us, "So be alert [give strict attention, be cautious and active in faith], for you do not know which day [whether near or far] your Lord is coming."

To steal the words from Aaron Rodgers, "There'll be a time when we meet that future, and right now, I'm just going to enjoy the present."

I'm Bryce Johnson, and you can *UNPACK* that!

PRAYER

Heavenly Father, I know I have much to be thankful for in this moment. Please help me to enjoy the present instead of worrying about the future. I know my future is in Your hands, and I trust in Your plan for my life. In Jesus' name, I pray. Amen.

How has focusing too much on the future caused you to miss out in the past?

How would intentionally thinking about the future hope that awaits you in heaven impact the way that you live your life now?

How does worrying too much about future concerns on earth demonstrate a lack of faith and trust in God and negatively affect the present?

DID YOU KNOW

Green Bay is the smallest major league professional sports market in America, but the franchise is consistently ranked in the top half of the most valuable in the NFL.

Day Twenty-Two: Coachability

Atlanta Falcons

During his accomplished career as an NFL quarterback, former Atlanta Falcons signal caller Matt Ryan won a league MVP award, was named to four Pro Bowls, and threw for over 62,000 yards while completing 65.6% of his passing attempts.

As he entered the back end of his career, there were no real questions about Ryan's ability to perform on the gridiron.

Heading into the 2021 season, however, there were some questions about how Ryan would adapt to life without his long-time wide receiver Julio Jones and with a brand-new head coach in Arthur Smith.

Having put together an accomplished and consistent career, Ryan could easily have been leery of listening to a new coach in his 14th season.

However, rather than being arrogant or stubborn, Ryan wanted to improve, learn, and grow.

Falcons head coach Arthur Smith said via *The Atlanta Journal-Constitution*, "Matt wants to be coached, and that's what I love about the guy. He's going into year 14, and he wants to be coached. The great players, they want to be coached...I certainly don't think I have all of the answers, and Matt certainly doesn't think he has all of the answers, so it's great dialogue."[1]

---

1. https://heavy.com/sports/nfl/atlanta-falcons/arthur-smith-matt-ryan-offseason-sync/

"Coachability" is a key difference between good and great athletes and this principle is not only crucial in sports but is just as valuable in our own lives.

Whether receiving instruction or constructive criticism from a boss, teacher, mentor, coach, pastor, parent, or friend, we can learn, grow, and improve if we're "coachable."

On the other hand, it's detrimental when we think we have all the answers, have everything figured out, and aren't willing to submit to the wisdom and knowledge of others.

When growing in our faith, we should be extremely passionate about having a "coachable" spirit and learning from those following Jesus closely and consistently.

Placing ourselves under solid leaders who can help guide us and speak wisdom into our lives is worthwhile. A deep sense of humility and hunger are also required, as well as acknowledging that we don't know everything.

The best instruction is rooted in biblical teaching and can encourage us in "coachability." The following three verses explain the importance of acquiring knowledge and seeking wisdom:

- "The fear of the Lord is the beginning of knowledge; fools despise wisdom and instruction." Proverbs 1:7 (ESV)

- "Give instruction to a wise man, and he will be still wiser; teach a righteous man, and he will increase in learning." Proverbs 9:9 (ESV)

- "An intelligent heart acquires knowledge, and the ear of the wise seeks knowledge." Proverbs 18:15 (ESV)

Matt Ryan was a veteran quarterback, but he was still leaning on his coaches and was learning from them.

Today, let's be encouraged that we're never too old or accomplished to embrace the knowledge and wisdom available from others.

I'm Bryce Johnson, and you can *UNPACK* that!

PRAYER

Heavenly Father, please give me a humble and coachable spirit so that I can continue to grow as a follower of Jesus, spouse, parent, and friend. Show me how to have a heart that desires knowledge and wisdom rooted in You and listen to leaders through whom You speak. Help me to hear You clearly, and thank you for being my ultimate coach. In Jesus' name, I pray. Amen.

When do you find it most difficult to receive correction or instruction from others?

How would your life look different if you had embraced all of the positive help and correction that was offered to you in the past?

Who are some people in your life that you might seek out for wisdom, counsel, and teaching?

DID YOU KNOW

The Falcons hold the record for the fewest points allowed per game in a season during the modern era, giving up only 9.2 points per contest in 1977.

Day Twenty-Three: Shutting Down the Star Power

Patrick Peterson was one of the best defensive players in the NFL during his prime, making the Pro Bowl in each of his first eight seasons with the Arizona Cardinals.

As a top cornerback, he did a tremendous job of limiting the other team's best wide receiver from having big games against him. But when shutting receivers down, something else took place.

Dan Bickley from AZCentral.com wrote, "As [Peterson's] mastered the art of his position, he has effectively shut down his own star power. He was the least-targeted NFL cornerback in 2016, with a ball thrown in his direction once every 8.5 passes. He rarely gets the opportunity to make the highlight reel, a hard concession for a player who relishes the limelight."

During his time in Arizona, Peterson was an outstanding athlete who could make big plays if the quarterback dared to throw the ball his way. But by keeping the ball away from receivers, he missed out on opportunities to intercept passes.

ProFootballTalk.com once used this headline in an article: "Patrick Peterson Has Performed His Way Into Obscurity."[1]

---

1.   shttps://www.nbcsports.com/nfl/profootballtalk/rumor-mill/news/patrick-peterson-has-performed-his-way-into-obscurity

In reality, Peterson's strong play didn't lead to the same attention that other cornerbacks might get for making highlight plays. A shutdown corner gets the job done quietly and with much less fanfare.

Even beyond football, many people enjoy making the "highlight reel" on social media, at work, in church, or in their community. It's a struggle to serve in obscurity instead of out front where people notice our "big plays."

Sure, sometimes people can be inspired and challenged by seeing how others serve and be encouraged by hearing stories about people's generosity. However, we're missing the point when our main motive is to seek the limelight or receive praise and personal gain from serving and giving.

As followers of Jesus, He calls us to a different approach and warns us about doing good for others to see.

Jesus says in Matthew 6:1-4 (ESV), "Beware of practicing your righteousness before other people in order to be seen by them, for then you will have no reward from your Father who is in heaven. Thus, when you give to the needy, sound no trumpet before you, as the hypocrites do in the synagogues and in the streets, that they may be praised by others. Truly, I say to you, they have received their reward. But when you give to the needy, do not let your left hand know what your right hand is doing, so that your giving may be in secret. And your Father who sees in secret will reward you."

It's one thing for athletes to desire the limelight and a highlight reel, but when we make "big plays," it should be because we are serving God for His glory.

Today, let's be okay with shutting down our "star power" to serve in obscurity for God's glory.

I'm Bryce Johnson, and you can *UNPACK* that!

PRAYER

Heavenly Father, I like to get credit for doing something good. Please help me realize when I am being prideful and selfish. I pray I will give and serve in secret, without doing it for the limelight and praise of others. I need Your strength to do so humbly. In Jesus' name, I pray. Amen.

What are some unhealthy ways that you have sought to gain the attention of others in your life?

How can you grow to become more content with not being recognized for the good things that you have done?

How would not needing to be recognized by others allow you to live with more peace and freedom?

DID YOU KNOW

The Cardinals are the oldest continuously run football franchise, having formed as the Morgan Athletic Club all the way back in 1898.

Day Twenty-Four:
Spiritual Toughness

Every year during training camp and the preseason, coaches and fans are excited to see what their new crop of rookies can do on the field.

But for as much excitement as the fans might have about their team's new players, most rookies take time to adapt to the game's speed and adjust to each play's physicality. Many either hit a wall or battle nagging injuries at some point during the season.

Baltimore Ravens head coach John Harbaugh made this candid observation about rookies at a press conference during a past training camp: "One thing I've noticed, guys coming out of college aren't as callused up as they used to be. There's a certain type of 'in shape,' certain type of football fitness, certain type of callousness—muscles, joints, tendons, ligaments—that kind of toughen up. They callus up a little bit, and you can practice all day and run all day. Then our guys coming in right now, most of them don't have that."

In contrast, Harbaugh described his veteran tight ends by saying: "They're not batting an eye. Why? Because they're callused up because they know how to practice because their bodies are just tougher. There's a physical toughness to it. They're mentally tough."[1]

Of course, football players must be tough, so it makes sense that those with built-up calluses from rigorous practice, intense training,

1. https://www.espn.com/nfl/story/_/id/24177013/baltimore-ravens-coach-john-har-baugh-says-rookies-tough-were-past

and challenging experiences can handle more than those who are more inexperienced or unprepared.

This illustration of toughness profoundly parallels our spiritual lives. As we go through battles that test our faith, God uses these experiences to build our spiritual toughness. The more we rely on God's strength during difficult times of "practice" and "training," the more valuable "calluses" we develop.

James 1:3 (AMP) explains, "Be assured that the testing of your faith [through experience] produces endurance [leading to spiritual maturity, and inner peace]."

Although it's challenging to endure phases that might feel like "training camp," we can trust in God's guidance through our trials and even celebrate that something positive is happening within us.

Romans 5:3-4 (NLT) offers this encouragement: "We can rejoice, too, when we run into problems and trials, for we know that they help us develop endurance. And endurance develops strength of character, and character strengthens our confident hope of salvation."

As we desire to deepen and strengthen our faith in Jesus so we can do the work of the Lord, we must experience whatever is required to gain spiritual toughness and become more like Him.

We learn that He is trustworthy, faithful, and empowering as each trial prepares us and develops us for the subsequent trial as we uniquely grow and change.

Today, let's not stay spiritually soft by sitting on the sidelines. Instead, let's embrace the challenges before us by trusting God to use them for our good and His purposes.

I'm Bryce Johnson, and you can *UNPACK* that!

PRAYER

Heavenly Father, thank you for using the hard times in my life to toughen me up spiritually. Help me to bring You glory as You use these challenges to build my faith and prepare me to handle even more. In Jesus' name, I pray. Amen.

How have you developed and matured because of past trials and challenges you have faced?

How do you think you might be able to learn to embrace trials and suffering in your life?

How can you ensure that you are taking advantage of the opportunity for growth that is present when you go through challenging times?

DID YOU KNOW

Through the 2024 season, the Ravens have had only three head coaches in franchise history: Ted Marchibroda, Brian Billick, and John Harbaugh.

Day Twenty-Five: "Keep Pounding"

Carolina Panthers

Though former Panthers and Saints linebacker Sam Mills stood just 5' 9" and was undrafted out of Montclair State, he overcame the odds by stringing together a successful professional career culminating with his election into the Pro Football Hall of Fame.

But despite overcoming the odds on the gridiron, Mills died in 2005 at the age of 45.

His widow, Melanie, gave the induction speech during the enshrinement ceremony, saying, "He was a father, a friend, a husband, and a leader who always kept pounding, no matter the odds."[1]

Mills was known as a player and a man who never gave up and didn't complain or make excuses, and his attitude and mindset continue to inspire us to overcome, have courage, and "keep pounding."

This mantra of "keep pounding" is credited to Mills and has been adopted by the Carolina Panthers organization and the entire fan base.

In the summer of 2003, Sam Mills was an assistant coach with the Carolina Panthers and was diagnosed with an aggressive form of intestinal cancer and given only a few months to live.

However, he continued coaching, and on the day before the Panthers hosted a playoff game against the Cowboys, Mills spoke to the team after practice.

---

1. https://www.usatoday.com/story/sports/nfl/2022/08/06/pro-football-hall-of-fame-enshrinement-speech-sam-mills-panthers-saints-usfl/10257212002/

According to Darin Gantt's article, "The Day Keep Pounding Was Born" (on Panthers.com), Mills' teammates remember him saying, "When I found out I had cancer, there were two things I could do: quit or keep pounding. I'm a fighter. I kept pounding. You're fighters, too. Keep pounding!"[2]

That memorable speech and phrase, "keep pounding," not only contributed to the team beating the Cowboys 29-10 the following night but provided inspiration leading them to the Super Bowl.

We all encounter daily challenges and lifelong obstacles, and there are countless situations where we choose to "keep pounding" or give up.

As followers of Jesus, we have an enemy that wants us to lose hope, be discouraged, be overcome with worry and doubts, and give up our faith. However, we must "keep pounding!"

In 1 Timothy 6:11-12 (NLT), Paul gives Timothy a similar plea: "But you, Timothy, are a man of God; so run from all these evil things. Pursue righteousness and a godly life, along with faith, love, perseverance, and gentleness. Fight the good fight for the true faith. Hold tightly to the eternal life to which God has called you, which you have declared so well before many witnesses."

No matter what we face, we must cling to Jesus, relying on His strength to help us fight the good fight of faith as we place our hope in His promises and eternal life in Him. As long as God still has us here, we must finish strong while persevering with faith and inspiring others to do the same.

Today, let's be encouraged to keep praying, trusting, obeying, seeking Him first...and "keep pounding" as we yield to the power of the Holy Spirit.

I'm Bryce Johnson, and you can *UNPACK* that!

---

2. https://www.panthers.com/news/sam-mills-keep-pounding-message-leaves-lasting-impact-on-atrium-health

PRAYER

Heavenly Father, there are days I want to give up, and I don't know how to keep going, but I know You are with me and love me. I need You, Your strength, and Your power within me to help me persevere. In Jesus' name, I pray. Amen.

What sorts of situations have tended to lead you towards discouragement in your life?

What biblical truths might serve to inspire you to continue persevering in your faith?

How would your life change if you demonstrated a greater willingness to fight and persevere?

DID YOU KNOW

The Panthers once lost 13 consecutive coin flips during the 2012 season. The odds of that happening were 1-in-8,192.

Day Twenty-Six: Consistency - 10,363 Straight

Throughout his tenure in the NFL with the Cleveland Browns, Hall of Fame offensive tackle Joe Thomas experienced unbelievable losses. According to the AP, Thomas' .287 winning percentage is the worst of any of the Hall of Fame's 369 inductees.

He also played for six different head coaches, never appeared in a playoff game, and blocked for 20 different starting quarterbacks—more than any other offensive lineman in NFL history.

Despite all the losses he endured within the Browns franchise, he remained reliable, steady, consistent, and committed by starting 167 of 167 games. Thomas started every game and played a record 10,363 consecutive snaps in his career—all with the Browns.

His wife, Annie Thomas, did an intro video before Joe's Hall of Fame induction speech and said, "He's the one you can rely on...His legacy is he is consistent. You can count on him no matter what."

Thomas then went on to say in his speech, "I want to start by quickly talking about a random number—10,363. That's not too random, but that's how many consecutive snaps I had during my career. That number 10,363 is special to me in a lot of ways, and not just because it's an NFL record but because it shows I was there for my brothers 10,363 times in a row. They could count on me. Being an offensive lineman is also about being a servant...Loyalty, consistency, doing something bigger than yourself, showing up for the man next to you. Those are the values I learned at an early age, and those are the values that I took onto the football field."

We can appreciate Joe Thomas' loyalty and steady nature—especially amid "losing seasons." The question is, are we that person for others?

Of course, nobody is perfect, and we disappoint people, but are we committed to serving those around us "play after play after play"?

It's fair to say that Joe's commitment and consistency revealed his love for his teammates, the game of football, and the fans of Cleveland.

When it comes to our lives as followers of Jesus, our love must drive us to show up for others and be committed to serving them.

Jesus says in John 15:12 (AMP), "This is My commandment, that you love and unselfishly seek the best for one another, just as I have loved you."

Because of our victory in Christ and His power within us, we can serve God and others consistently and with commitment every day.

In 1 Corinthians 15:58 (CSB), Paul writes, "Therefore, my dear brothers and sisters, be steadfast, immovable, always excelling in the Lord's work, because you know that your labor in the Lord is not in vain."

Today, let's be consistent with our prayers, worship, fellowship, and reading of God's Word so that we can be committed to being there for others.

I'm Bryce Johnson, and you can *UNPACK* that!

PRAYER

Heavenly Father, I desire to be the person who shows up for others. Please empower me to be a consistent friend, remain steadfast in my faith, and be committed to serving those around me. I need Your help to do so. In Jesus' name, I pray. Amen.

How have you been positively impacted by the loyalty of others in your life?

Who are some people in your life that you can commit to serve consistently?

How will you be able to continue to serve someone consistently even if they are not responding in the way you desire?

DID YOU KNOW

Former Browns head coach Paul Brown is credited with inventing the modern face mask, practice squads, and draw plays, amongst his other innovations.

Day Twenty-Seven: "It Would Be Obscene"

Every NFL team would love to win the Super Bowl, and even those who have already won still desire to win again. As an owner, Jerry Jones has seen his beloved Dallas Cowboys win three Super Bowls, but the last time it occurred was in 1996.

Knowing the thrill of holding up the Lombardi Trophy and winning the NFL's biggest prize, Jones hopes his team will unite to bring the Cowboys back to Super Bowl contention.

Jones has been so ready to win again that he once told 105.3 The Fan in Dallas, "It would be embarrassing, it would be shocking if you knew the size of the check I would write if it guaranteed me a Super Bowl. It would be obscene. There is nothing I would do financially not to get a Super Bowl."[1]

Jones is willing to pay any price to get another ring and is prepared to give up whatever it takes to have what he wants, (but unfortunately for him that's not an option).

As Jones speaks in the context of winning a significant prize in football, Jesus describes the more remarkable value of God's kingdom in His parables in Matthew 13:44-46 (NIV): "The kingdom of heaven is like treasure hidden in a field. When a man found it, he hid it again, and then in his joy went and sold all he had and bought that field. Again, the kingdom of heaven is like a merchant looking

1. https://www.nfl.com/news/jerry-jones-would-write-embarrassing-check-for-title-0ap3000000951918

for fine pearls. When he found one of great value, he went away and sold everything he had and bought it."

These are beautiful reminders that when we know God and experience the kingdom of heaven through Jesus' grace and redemption, it's worth giving up everything else to have Him.

Jesus is our prize, and the value and joy of being in heaven's kingdom are better than anything else. All that matters is to know Him, follow Him, and be with Him no matter the cost.

Today, let's ask ourselves how much we value God and the kingdom of heaven. Do we treasure Him and place nothing above Him in importance? Are we willing to sacrifice and surrender to have Him? Do we have a willingness similar to Jerry Jones and his passion for another Super Bowl ring? Would it be "shocking" and "obscene" for people to know what we'd be willing to part with in obedience to God?

God will probably not ask us for a billion dollars, but He wants our heart and devotion. Today, let's ensure we aren't holding onto anything we need to let go of to experience the fullness of joy and peace we find in Him.

I'm Bryce Johnson, and you can *UNPACK* that!

PRAYER

Heavenly Father, help me have more of a perspective like the man and merchant willing to give up everything. I pray You'll help me not hold back from fully embracing all You are and have made available to me through Jesus. It's in His name I pray. Amen.

What things in your life tend to impede upon you giving your full devotion to God?

What steps can you take to grow in your understanding of how valuable your relationship with God is?

What sacrifices might you be able to make in order to ensure that you are consistently growing in your relationship with God?

DID YOU KNOW

The Cowboys record for single-season rushing yards is held by DeMarco Murray, who rushed for 1,845 yards during the 2014 season.

Day Twenty-Eight: The Bengals' Key to Success

The Cincinnati Bengals surprised many people in the football world by making it all the way to Super Bowl LVI.

But how did they get there, and what was their secret to success? The answer to that question seems to center around the team being selfless.

Bengals quarterback Joe Burrow shared this about his team's multiple playmakers (including Ja'Marr Chase, Tee Higgins, Tyler Boyd, and Joe Mixon): "Everyone knows how good they are as players, but not everyone knows how good they are as people...really unselfish guys that don't care who gets the shine."[1]

Also, former NFL cornerback DeAngelo Hall explained on NFL Network that head coach Zac Taylor isn't only leading an unselfish team but is an example of a selfless leader.

Hall said, "You know the thing that's really impressed me most about Zac Taylor is really his selflessness. When you think about the way he leads this football team, it's not about him, it's not about taking credit or getting credit, and I think you see that in the way the team rallies behind him, rallies behind everyone in that locker

---

1. https://x.com/NFLonCBS/status/1467528425862832135

room. To me, when you have that kinda dynamic going on in your building, that's how you win."[2]

Seeing a team like the Bengals demonstrate selflessness is an excellent example of what that attitude can accomplish.

What about us? Are we focused on our own stats while making sure we get to shine and receive the credit? Or are we following Jesus and asking Him to transform our selfishness into selflessness by valuing the interests of others more than ourselves?

Unfortunately, becoming selfless is challenging because the world teaches us to look out for "number one" and ensure we "get ours." But the Bible teaches us a different approach, leading to much more winning. Philippians 2:3-4 (ESV) says, "Do nothing from selfish ambition or conceit, but in humility count others more significant than yourselves. Let each of you look not only to his own interests, but also to the interests of others."

On the flip side, whether in sports or life, when there's selfishness and a dominant me-focus, we see significant problems and the inability to win.

As the Bible says in James 3:16 (NLT), "For wherever there is jealousy and selfish ambition, there you will find disorder and evil of every kind."

Today, let's ask God to reveal the selfishness in our lives and allow Him to help us become less me-focused so we'll be willing to let our "teammates" shine, celebrate others, and "block" for one another. Let's enjoy the blessings of living an unselfish life as we choose to be more like Jesus, whose selflessness gives us life.

I'm Bryce Johnson, and you can *UNPACK* that!

---

2. https://firstsportz.com/nfl-deangelo-hall-reveals-this-is-what-impressed-him-most-about-zac-taylor-the-bengals-head-coach-that-will-win-them-the-super-bowl/

PRAYER

Heavenly Father, I confess I can be selfish, but I desire to be more like Jesus. Please help me lay down my selfish ambitions, value others more, build them up, and love them. I pray you'll remove my ego and show me how to be more selfless. In Jesus' name, I pray. Amen.

How has your selfishness negatively impacted you in the past?

In which areas of your life do you tend to demonstrate the greatest amount of selfishness?

What action can you commit to taking to become more selfless in the way that you live?

DID YOU KNOW

Former Bengals head coach Sam Wyche was the first coach in NFL history to utilize the no-huddle as his base offense.

Day Twenty-Nine: Bears Are Looking for "The Grizzly"

Every NFL team has a unique process and approach to identifying the specific types of players they want to draft. Ahead of the 2024 NFL Draft, the Chicago Bears utilized a particularly clever way of documenting the players who possessed the qualities they desired.

In an article on nbcsportschicago.com, writer Alex Shapiro explained what the Bears did: "If a player exhibits all the traits they want, regardless of whether that player has a first-round grade or a seventh-round grade, the team puts a little Bears head icon on their tag."

Bears GM Ryan Poles explained further: "We call them the Grizzly…the top Bear. They've got to impact the football team from a skillset standpoint, but we always are gonna look at some key things when we talk about passion for the game, coachability, dependability, resilience."[1]

With countless talented players with similar football abilities available, it makes sense that the intangibles or characteristics a team values the most will be the differentiator.

While the Bears were looking to draft a "Grizzly" who had "passion for the game, coachability, dependability, and resilience," those

---

1.   https://www.nbcchicago.com/news/sports/nfl/chicago-bears/how-bears-identify-grizzlies-in-the-2024-nfl-draft-and-why-its-important-to-their-evaluations/3418569/

characteristics should be differentiators even more so in our own lives as we follow Jesus.

When others "scout" us, they should see our "passion for God"—because we take seriously the words of Jesus in Mark 12:30 (ESV): "'And you shall love the Lord your God with all your heart and with all your soul and with all your mind and with all your strength.'"

They should notice our "coachability" and identify our desire to grow, learn, and receive teaching from God's Word. Jesus tells us in Mark 4:25 (AMP), "For whoever has [a teachable heart], to him more [understanding] will be given; and whoever does not have [a yearning for truth], even what he has will be taken away from him."

They should also see evidence of our "dependability." Even though we aren't perfect, we should be relied on to do what we say and be trusted to seek to live like Jesus. The Bible challenges us in 1 John 2:5-6 (NLT): "But those who obey God's Word truly show how completely they love Him. That is how we know we are living in Him. Those who say they live in God should live their lives as Jesus did."

Lastly, our "resilience" should be recognized as we demonstrate how we depend on God to help us overcome challenges. We follow the example of Paul as he writes in 2 Corinthians 4:8-10 (NLT), "We are pressed on every side by troubles, but we are not crushed. We are perplexed, but not driven to despair. We are hunted down, but never abandoned by God. We get knocked down, but we are not destroyed."

Today, let's remember that the characteristics of "The Grizzly" are the same ones that allow us to glorify God.

Let's continue to value and demonstrate our passion for God, coachability, dependability, and resilience as we walk with Jesus.

I'm Bryce Johnson, and you can *UNPACK* that!

PRAYER

Heavenly Father, I desire to become more like Jesus and live a life that honors You. Please help me passionately live for You and be coachable and teachable as I seek to understand Your Word. I pray you'll strengthen me to be dependable and resilient, regardless of my circumstances. In Jesus' name, I pray. Amen.

If other people were asked about the passion that you demonstrate for God, how do you think they would respond?

What steps can you take in your life to grow in your passion and commitment to the Lord?

When do you tend to find it difficult to be resilient in your faith?

DID YOU KNOW

George Halas purchased the rights to the Bears franchise in 1921 for just $100.

Day Thirty: The Bills' Despair

Having lost to the Kansas City Chiefs in two of the previous three postseasons, many Buffalo Bills fans were excited to get another crack at their rivals in the 2024 divisional round.

Unlike the previous postseason matchups in the season prior, the 2024 contest would be the first time Buffalo hosted the game.

The Bills needed to win, and considering how well they had been playing and how incredible their turnaround was during the regular season, it appeared things were lining up for them to beat the Chiefs in front of the loyal "Bills Mafia."

Unfortunately for Bills fans, a missed field goal, key dropped passes, a failed fake punt, and a defense decimated by injuries ultimately led to a heartbreaking 27-24 loss.

Buffalo had opportunities, and the result may have been different if a few plays went their way. Instead, fans felt despair, as it was the third time in four years the Chiefs knocked them out of the playoffs.

Understandably, Bills fans responded to the heartbreaking loss with anguish, misery, and gloom for having watched their team go another season without the Super Bowl win they desperately wanted to experience.

Despite their real emotions, we also know that it's just sports and that many people today wake up with immense despair and anguish about significant life situations. Misery and gloom are pres-

117

ent because of broken relationships, a demanding job status, the devastating loss of a loved one, a health diagnosis, or countless other heartbreaking outcomes.

Whether in sports or life, despair takes over when hope disappears. Yet, as followers of Jesus, we don't have to let misery, gloom, and anguish dominate our emotions and outlook.

When we find ourselves consumed by pain, unhappiness, and discouragement, we must always turn to the Lord and allow Him to meet us in that place.

Psalm 34:17-19 (NLT) tells us, "The Lord hears His people when they call to Him for help. He rescues them from all their troubles. The Lord is close to the brokenhearted; He rescues those whose spirits are crushed. The righteous person faces many troubles, but the Lord comes to the rescue each time."

When we find ourselves filled with the despair that comes from life's problems, we must ask as the psalmist does in Psalm 43:5 (AMP): "Why are you in despair, O my soul? And why are you restless and disturbed within me?"

As the psalmist continues, we must also remind ourselves, "Hope in God and wait expectantly for Him, for I shall again praise Him, The help of my [sad] countenance and my God."

When we face the losses of life, we can't let despair win. Instead, let's keep our hope in the One who heals, comforts, and rescues.

I'm Bryce Johnson, and you can *UNPACK* that!

PRAYER

Heavenly Father, please pull me out of my despair and anguish and help me hope in You. I know You are near, and I know that You care. Thank you for being willing to rescue me and heal me. I pray You work mightily in me, and please help me worship You through the pain. In Jesus' name, I pray. Amen.

When do you tend to find it the most difficult to live with joy, hope, and trust?

What do you think it would practically look like for you to fully put your hope in God at all times?

In what ways has despair impacted your life in the past?

DID YOU KNOW

The Bills hold the record for the largest comeback in postseason history, coming back from a 35-3 deficit to defeat the Houston Oilers in 1993.

Day Thirty-One: Giving Up Control of the Play-Calling

The Denver Broncos were one of the most disappointing teams in the NFL in 2022. They finished the year with a 5-12 record and ranked last in the league offensively in points scored.

During that season, Nathaniel Hackett was in his first year as head coach of the Broncos, following his role as Green Bay's offensive coordinator from 2019-2021. Although he didn't call plays for the Packers, he previously did for the Bills and the Jaguars. Only one of his offenses ranked high in scoring during those five seasons of play-calling.

Starting with the Broncos, he served as the head coach and the play-caller for an offense that had difficulty scoring touchdowns.

But despite the offensive woes, Hackett announced halfway through the season that he was not planning to give up play-calling duties. He said, "Right now, on a short week, we're going to keep the status quo."[1]

It's pretty fair to question his unwillingness to cede control of the offense, and it would probably have been wise for him to hand over the reins considering his efforts were clearly not working.

---

1. https://larrybrownsports.com/football/broncos-coach-nathaniel-hackett-play-call-ing/604344

When it comes to our lives, we can also have a tough time handing over the reins. We like to be in charge and call the plays.

The problem is, when we're unwilling to cede control and hand over the reins to Jesus, our lives ultimately flounder. Our pride and stubbornness cause continued "offensive woes" as we "keep the status quo."

So we must ask ourselves, who is "calling the plays"? Who is in charge of guiding our "offense"?

Thankfully, God knows what He's doing and deserves our trust so we can freely give Him our "play-calling" responsibilities.

Psalm 32:8-11 (NLT) tells us, "The Lord says, 'I will guide you along the best pathway for your life. I will advise you and watch over you. Do not be like a senseless horse or mule that needs a bit and bridle to keep it under control.' Many sorrows come to the wicked, but unfailing love surrounds those who trust the Lord. So rejoice in the Lord and be glad, all you who obey Him! Shout for joy, all you whose hearts are pure!"

Each day, let's be willing to surrender to His guidance and His direction as we step aside in humble submission to His game plan. Let's seek Him for wisdom in decision-making so we can confidently know He will make the best call in each situation we face in life.

Psalm 37:23-24 (AMP) says, "The steps of a [good and righteous] man are directed and established by the Lord, And He delights in his way [and blesses his path]. When he falls, he will not be hurled down, Because the Lord is the One who holds his hand and sustains him."

I'm Bryce Johnson, and you can *UNPACK* that!

PRAYER

Heavenly Father, forgive me for trying to control everything and thinking that I know what's best. Forgive me for my pride and stubbornness. I pray that You show me Your will, help me to follow Your path, and guide me to make wise decisions. I surrender to You, Jesus, and submit to Your ways. In Your name, I pray, Jesus. Amen.

In what areas of your life do you find it most difficult to let God be in control?

What might your lack of surrendering to God in certain areas reveal about what is going on in your heart?

What do you think it would look like for you to fully surrender and let God be in control of your life?

DID YOU KNOW

The Broncos were the first AFL team to defeat an NFL team, topping the Detroit Lions 13-7 in 1967.

Day Thirty-Two: Not the "Same Old Lions"

As a franchise, the Detroit Lions have historically been losers, and the saying "Same Old Lions" symbolizes the team's history of frustration.

However, dropping that label began on June 23, 2020, when Sheila Hamp became the principal owner of the Lions, taking over for her mother, Martha Ford. Hamp hired Chris Spielman to the front office, Brad Holmes as general manager, and Dan Campbell as head coach.

Together, they changed the Detroit Lions' identity, eventually leading the franchise to the 2023 NFC Championship Game.

As head coach, Dan Campbell took over—he changed the team's approach, mindset, and their belief that they could move past the history of losing and who they used to be. The players believed this truth and demonstrated on a huge stage that they were now the new Lions.

In sports and life, identity is often discussed and defined as "the characteristics that make up who or what you are." Identity "refers to our sense of who we are as individuals and as members of social groups...and our sense of how others may perceive and label us."[1]

The Lions' identity changed, which means the way they play, what they believe to be true, the results and how others view them are now different.

---

1. facinghistory.org/resource-library/exploring-concept-identity

When we surrender our lives to Jesus, we experience a much deeper and critical identity change. We move from "same old ___" who can't seem to win, full of disappointment and old patterns of sin, to ultimately become a new creation.

2 Corinthians 5:17 (AMP) explains, "Therefore if anyone is in Christ [that is, grafted in, joined to Him by faith in Him as Savior], he is a new creature [reborn and renewed by the Holy Spirit]; the old things [the previous moral and spiritual condition] have passed away. Behold, new things have come [because spiritual awakening brings a new life]."

The question becomes, do we believe that our identity has changed? Do we acknowledge we are now God's child, declared forgiven, more than conquerors, a member of the body of Christ, and freed from the bondage of sin?

When Jesus takes over, our lives and identity are rooted in Him. He then changes our approach and mindset and helps us believe we can move past our history of losing and who we used to be. When our identity is in Christ, the way we "play," what we believe to be true, the results, and how others view us are also different.

Today, let's remember that if we are in Christ, we base our identity on who He is, what He's done for us, and who He says we are because we are no longer the "Same Old Lions"!

I'm Bryce Johnson, and you can *UNPACK* that!

PRAYER

Heavenly Father, I'm so thankful that I have been made new through Christ. I pray You help me believe and understand that my identity has changed and I'm not who I used to be. I pray You continue to transform me, and when people see me, they see Jesus shining through. In Jesus' name, I pray. Amen.

Outside of your relationship with Christ, where are some places that you have attempted to find your identity in the past?

How might rooting your identity completely in Christ help you to be more steady and consistent in the way that you live?

How have you practically experienced being a new creation in Christ?

DID YOU KNOW

Legendary musician Marvin Gaye unsuccessfully tried out for the Lions in 1970.

NEXT STEPS

Connect with the UNPACKIN' it Community of sports fans following Jesus!

Enjoy more devotionals and other content from UN-PACKIN' it Ministries.

www.unpackinit.com

I hope this book challenged, encouraged, and inspired you to follow Jesus and become more like Him. It's my prayer that you would pass the book along to others and get copies for your friends and family.

As you continue in your faith journey, I hope you will connect with UNPACKIN' it Ministries, a ministry for sports fans that began in 2014. In addition to this book of devotionals, we also send new faith and sports devotionals out Monday, Wednesday, and Friday through email. We unpack spiritual truths and relatable parallels from the sports world to help readers grow in their faith. Each day's devotional focuses on relevant scripture and closes with a short prayer.

*Subscribe TODAY at unpackinit.com/subscribe.

UNPACKIN' it Ministries offers numerous five-day reading plans on the popular Bible reading app. While unpacking sports through a lens of faith and Biblical truth, you'll be challenged, encouraged, and inspired as a sports fan to follow Jesus and become more like Him.

*Download the YouVersion app on your mobile device and search for "UNPACKIN' it."

We also offer opportunities for sports fans to experience fellowship through gatherings, small groups, and events. I invite you to get involved with our other ministry initiatives which include Fantasy Football Fellowship and Sports Fan Fellowship.

Another way our ministry uses sports parallels that relate to life and faith is through conversations on *The UNPACKIN' it Podcast* which can be watched on YouTube and social media or listened to on any podcast platform. We unpack big sports stories, impactful faith journeys, and the ups and downs of life with intriguing athletes, coaches, media personalities, and ministry leaders.

*Subscribe using your favorite podcast platform or visit unpackinit.com/podcast.

My passion is to see sports fans everywhere following Jesus and doing so in community with other sports fans. Thanks for reading this book…to God be all the glory, honor and praise!

Facebook.com/unpackinit

youtube.com/unpackinit

Let us know how God moved in your life while reading this book by emailing Bryce@thesportsdevotional.com.

A Sports Fan's Prayer

I *pray that I put more faith in Jesus
than in my favorite player.*

I *pray that I have more passion for sharing the gospel
than celebrating a championship win.*

I *pray that I find more joy in Christ
than in seeing my team score in the final seconds of a game.*

I *pray that I am more committed to following Jesus
than stats and scores.*

I *pray that I place more trust in God's Word
than in sports media.*

I *pray that I'm more dedicated to my family and friends
than watching my favorite team play.*

I *pray that I have peace that surpasses all understanding
even during a losing season.*

I *pray that I get angrier about injustice in the world
than I do about a ref's bad call.*

I *pray that I believe God is a God of miracles
even beyond the court and field.*

I *pray that I embrace real winning
as receiving God's grace and forgiveness.*

In *Jesus' name, I watch and pray ... A M E N!*

SCAN HERE to learn more about
Invite Ministries—created to invite people to a deeper
faith and living relationship with Jesus Christ